‹GHANA›

MAJOR WORLD NATIONS

GHANA

Jeanie M. Barnett

CHELSEA HOUSE PUBLISHERS
Philadelphia

Chelsea House Publishers

Contributing Author: Derek Davis

Copyright © 1999 by Chelsea House Publishers,
a division of Main Line Book Co.
All rights reserved.
Printed and bound in the United States of America.

3   5   7   9   8   6   4   2

Library of Congress Cataloging-in-Publication Data

Barnett, Jeanie M.
Ghana / Jeanie M. Barnett.
p.   cm. — (Major world nations)
Includes index.
Summary: Surveys the history, topography, people, and culture of Ghana,
with emphasis on its current economy, industry, and place
in the political world.
ISBN 0–7910–4739–3 (hardcover)
1. Ghana—Juvenile literature.   [1. Ghana.]
I. Title.   II. Series.
DT510.B37   1997
966.7—dc21   97–23012
CIP
AC

◄CONTENTS►

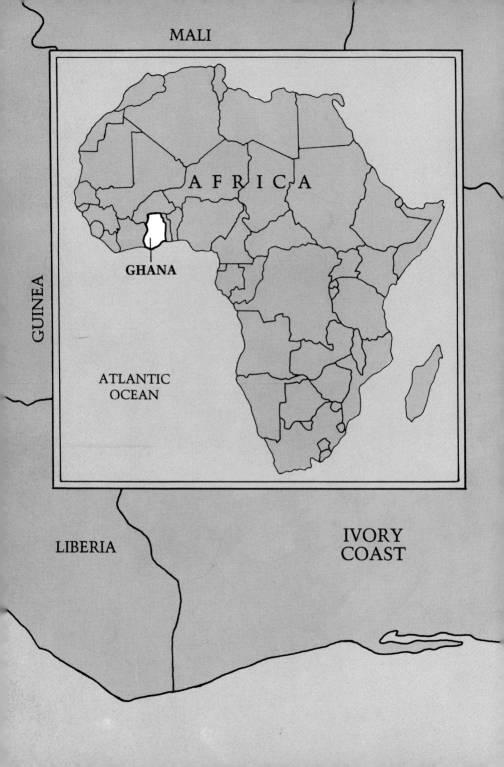

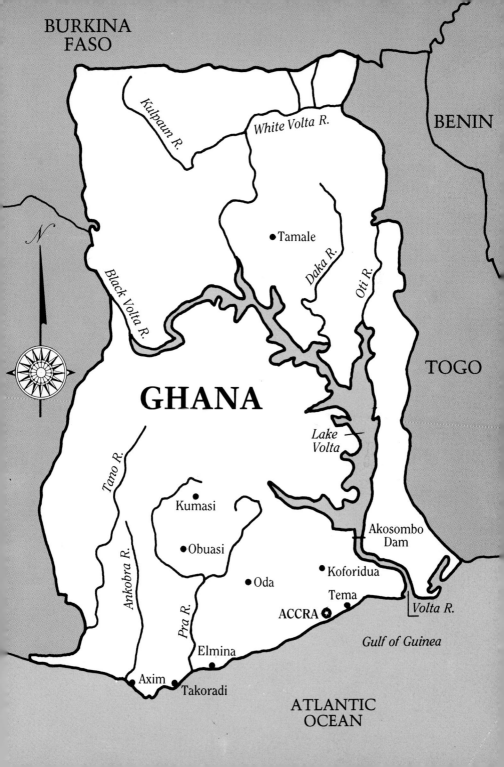

◄ FACTS AT A GLANCE ►

Land and People

Location	Western Africa, on the Atlantic Ocean's Gulf of Guinea, 400 miles (640 kilometers) north of the equator
Area	92,100 square miles (238,539 square kilometers)
Highest Point	Mount Afadjato, 2,905 feet (880 meters)
Climate	Tropical; mean temperature is between 70° and 90° Fahrenheit (21° and 32° Centigrade); annual rainfall is between 33 and 87 inches (838 and 2,210 millimeters)
Capital	Accra (population 950,000)
Major Cities	Kumasi (population 385,000); Tamale (population 151,000); Tema (population 121,000)
Population	17,700,000
Population Density	192 persons per square mile (74 per sq km)
Population Distribution	Urban, 36 percent; rural, 64 percent
Official Language	English
Other Languages	More than 50 ethnic languages
Religions	Traditional African Religions, 38 percent; Christian, 24 percent; Muslim, 30 percent
Major Ethnic Groups	Akan, Mossi-Dagomba, Ewe, Ga-Adangme

Economy

Major Resources	Gold, timber, diamonds, bauxite, manganese
Major Exports	Cocoa, gold, timber, ores
Gross Domestic Product	U.S. $8 billion
Per Capita Gross Domestic Product	Equal to U.S. $450
Percentage of Gross Domestic Product	Manufacturing and industry, 15 percent; trade, 25 percent; agriculture, 50 percent
Employment Statistics	Agriculture and fishing, 55 percent; industry, 19 percent; sales and clerical, 15 percent; professional, 3 percent; services, transportation, and communications, 8 percent
Currency	Cedi

Government

Form of Government	Parliamentary constitutional republic
Head of State and Government	President
Voting Rights	Universal suffrage

◄HISTORY AT A GLANCE►

about 10,000 B.C.	Hunter-gatherers drift south from the Western Sudan to the area that is now Ghana.
5500 to 2500 B.C.	Hunter-gatherers reach the Atlantic Ocean.
about 400 A.D.	Agricultural societies develop in the Western Sudan. Arab traders travel to the Western Sudan in search of gold and ivory.
1200 to 1300	The Mali Empire opens new gold mines in the forest regions of modern Ghana. The first permanent settlers—ancestors of modern Ghana's ethnic groups—arrive to work the gold mines.
1470	Portuguese traders in search of gold arrive on the coast of what is now Ghana. The Portuguese call the coast "Mina de Ouro" (Gold Mine).
1482	The Portuguese build Elmina Castle on the coast to protect their trade area.
1500s	Britain, France, and the Netherlands make their first trading voyages to the Gold Coast.
1600s	Slavery becomes the colony's most important trade activity.
1612	The Dutch begin construction of their own forts on the coast.
1637	The Dutch take control of Elmina Castle and other Portuguese forts along the Gold Coast.
1700 to 1800	The Akan and Asante tribes increase their power and wealth by aiding European slave traders.

1811 to 1874	The Asante and the British engage in several battles that culminate in the Sagrenti War of 1874. The Asante lose the war and sign the Treaty of Komena, giving up the Gold Coast south of the Pra and Ofin rivers. This area is made a British colony.
1816	The Dutch and the British sign trade treaties with the Asante.
1823	The British violate the treaty's terms. The Asante assassinate the British governor in neighboring Sierra Leone.
1830	The British government sends Captain George Maclean to administer Gold Coast trade.
1830 to 1842	The British sign peace treaties with several tribes.
1872	The Dutch leave the Gold Coast; the British become the ruling colonial power.
1901	The Asante surrender the remainder of their kingdom to the British.
1920	A group of Gold Coast Africans form the National Congress of British West Africa and demand political reforms, including steps that would lead to independence.
1947	The United Gold Coast Convention (UGCC) is formed. The UGCC's secretary general, Kwame Nkrumah, splits from the party to form the more radical Convention People's party (CPP).
1950	The colonial administration jails Nkrumah after the CPP stages a strike.
1951	Under pressure, the British call for elections of an all-African legislature to govern under British authority. The CPP wins a majority of the seats. Nkrumah is released from jail.
1956	Nkrumah pushes for self-government and com-

plete independence from Great Britain.

March 1957   The Gold Coast colony wins independence from British rule. The colony is renamed Ghana, and Nkrumah is sworn in as its first prime minister.

1960   Ghana adopts a new constitution, changing the government to a republican system with Nkrumah as president.

1960 to 1965   Export prices plummet and Ghana's economy slumps.

February 1966   Nkrumah is ousted in a coup. The National Liberation council (NLC), led by military officers, takes over.

October 1969   The NLC calls for elections and a return to civilian government. The Progress party wins a majority of seats in the Legislative Assembly. Progress party leader Kofia Busia is named prime minister.

January 1972   Colonel Ignatius Acheampong overthrows the civilian government. He installs the National

A woman and child collect water at wells dug into the bed of a dried-up pond.

A man pounds yams and plantains with the traditional mortar and pestle in preparation for the evening meal.

	Redemption council as Ghana's new ruling body.
July 1978	Lieutenant General Frederick Akuffo replaces Acheampong as head of the military government.
June 1979	Flight Lieutenant Jerry Rawlings seizes control of the government. He calls for elections in July.
September 1979	Following free elections in July, Rawlings steps down. Hilla Limann is sworn in as president and the country adopts a democratic constitution.
September 1979 to December 1981	Ghana's economic problems increase and the Limann administration loses credibility with the people.
December 1981	Rawlings returns to power.
April 1992	New democratic constitution granting suffrage, approved by referendum
December 1992	Rawlings elected president of Fourth Republic

Ghanaian drummers at a festival beat out rhythms that most likely accompany a traditional fable or story of the past.

Ghana and the World

In 1957, Ghana became the first African nation south of the Sahara Desert to win independence from a colonial power. The independence of this former British colony heralded the beginning of a new Africa. Free of colonial domination, Ghana held out the hope to other African colonies that independence would lead to growth and prosperity. Unfortunately, in the years since independence, Ghana—and many other African nations—have seen their hopes dashed by military governments, crop failures, and poor economic management.

Adversity and struggle are not new to Ghanaians. For almost 500 years they lived under the yoke of various European powers. In the 15th century, Portuguese trading ships sailing along the coast of West Africa discovered gold on a stretch of land between the mouths of the Tano and Volta rivers. The Portuguese called this stretch of land "Mina de Ouro" (Gold Mine). Within a short time the area became known as the Gold Coast (in 1957, the first government changed the colony's name to Ghana).

For five centuries the Gold Coast played a central role in the growth of world trade. At first, gold attracted the Europeans, but it was soon overshadowed by a more profitable commodity: slaves. Millions of Africans were taken from their homes and shipped across the Atlantic Ocean to work as slaves on plantations in the United States, the Caribbean, and Latin America. Ghana's coastline is dotted with the ruins of castles and forts built by European powers to protect their interests in the slave trade.

In the late 1800s, the European nations established colonies on the African continent. Great Britain made the Gold Coast a crown colony in 1874. When slavery was abolished in the late 19th century, the British established plantations to grow export crops such as sugarcane, tobacco, cotton, and cacao. The Gold Coast became the world's leading producer of cacao, the main ingredient in cocoa and chocolate. Even today, Ghana exports hundreds of thousands of tons of cocoa every year to candy manufacturers in Europe and the United States.

Ghana was the first African colony to develop an effective independence movement. The leader of that movement, Kwame Nkrumah, became the country's founding father and acted as president until 1966. His struggles with the British and calls for African independence inspired other independence movements across the continent.

Twins are generally regarded as good luck in West Africa. These twins in formal attire will be honored at a Ga Homowo festival.

Since independence, Ghana has struggled with political instability and economic woes. Yet, despite its problems, Ghana remains a peaceful country. The last war fought on Ghanaian soil took place when the Asante people rebelled against the British in 1901.

Today, more than 50 ethnic groups live in Ghana, each with its own language and traditions. Most Ghanaians live in small villages in the countryside and farm small plots of land. About one-third of the population lives in the country's major cities, which range from bustling, cosmopolitan Accra to traditional, open-air market centers like Kumasi.

The legacy of European colonialism, the effects of slavery, and the challenges of independence have shaped modern Ghana into one of the most interesting nations in Africa. The nations of Africa continue to watch Ghana and learn from its experiences.

Market vendors, the majority of whom are women, represent the most common business enterprise in West Africa—selling and trading food.

◄20►

The Land and Its People

The small nation of Ghana is located on the western coast of Africa, about 400 miles (640 kilometers) north of the equator. The Atlantic Ocean forms the country's southern border. Three French-speaking countries that were once colonies of France are located on Ghana's other borders: to the east is Togo; to the west is the Ivory Coast; and to the north is Burkina Faso (formerly Upper Volta).

Ghana's total land area is only 92,100 square miles (238,539 square kilometers), but within this small area are three distinct geographical regions: coast, forest, and savanna. In the south, sandy and rocky beaches cover the 340-mile (550-kilometer) Atlantic Ocean coastline. The Pra and Ankobra rivers, which drain the central portions of the country, weave through the sand dunes and hills on the coast until they reach the ocean. Many smaller rivers end in the coastal area without reaching the sea and form a series of salty marshes. Accra, the capital city of Ghana, is located on this coastal plain.

Sandy beach quickly turns to tropical forest as one moves north. This thick belt of forest covers almost one-third of Ghana; mahogany and teak, two hardwood trees especially prized for furniture-making and boat-building, grow in the forest region. The forest region also has concentrations of minerals, including the gold that brought Europeans to the country.

The eastern edge of the forest is punctuated by the Akwapim Hills, which have an average height of 1,500 feet (460 meters). Mount Afadjato, the highest point in Ghana (2,905 feet, or 885 m), is located in this range, which forms Ghana's border with Togo.

Farther north the forest tapers off into savanna, an area of dry, grassy plains with few trees. The most prominent feature in the northern region is the Gambaga Scarp, a series of 300- to 600-meter-high cliffs. The Black Volta and the White Volta rivers flow through this region and join together to the south to form the Volta River. The Volta was dammed in the early 1970s in order to provide hydroelectric power for the country. The Akosombo Dam project led to the creation of Lake Volta, the world's largest man-made lake. The lake has become Ghana's most conspicuous landmark, covering 3,371 square miles (8,730 square kilometers).

Even though it is close to the equator, the average temperature in Ghana is only between 70° and 90° Fahrenheit (21° and 32° Centigrade) year round. The humidity, however, ranges between 50 percent and 80 percent, which makes the lowland areas in the south especially oppressive. Annual rainfall ranges from 33 to 87 inches (838 to 2,210 millimeters), with the southern part of the country receiving more rain than the north.

The south receives more rain because the moist breezes of the Atlantic Ocean give the area two rainy seasons: April-July and September-November. Northern Ghana's climate is drier because of the harmattan, a northeasterly wind that blows into Ghana from the Sahara Desert each year. The harmattan lasts from November to April. While the wind makes the northern region cooler, it also dries up or greatly diminishes the water supplies in the north. A rainy season follows the harmattan, during which northern farmers plant and harvest their crops.

Over the years the northern area of the forest zone has been cleared of trees so farmers can grow plants. Most of Ghana's cereal crops, including maize (corn), sorghum, millet, and rice, are grown here. The area remains sparsely populated, however, because of the harsh harmattan.

In recent years the harmattan has created major food shortages in Ghana. In 1983, the harmattan blew across the entire country, delaying the rains in the south and causing a drought that lasted until the end of the year. Farmers were unable to grow their crops, and widespread starvation seemed imminent. Fortunately, foreign

A Hausa vendor at Makola marketplace sells prayer beads and other Muslim religious items from his stall.

countries responded to the government's pleas for food donations and famine—such as the one that afflicted Ethiopia—was avoided.

Ghana is divided into ten administrative regions: Ashanti, Brong-Ahafo, Central, Eastern, Greater Accra, Northern, Upper East, Upper West, Volta, and Western. Accra, Ghana's capital, is a coastal city that makes up the Greater Accra region. The Central, Western, Eastern, and Ashanti regions belong to Ghana's forest zone. Much of the forest in these regions has been cleared to allow the farming of crops such as cacao, Ghana's most important export.

Another productive area is the Akwapim Hills in the Eastern region. One of Ghana's most profitable export items, palm oil, is produced here. Diamonds are also mined in the Eastern region. The most important diamond-mining center is Oda, a town on the northern side of the Akwapim Hills. Gold is mined at Obuasi, a town south of Kumasi in the Ashanti region.

The Upper East, Upper West, Brong-Ahafo, and Northern regions are located in the northern part of Ghana. Although these regions are important for cereal crops, they are sparsely populated because of the harsh, dry environment; in fact, these four regions account for only 25 percent of Ghana's population.

An Ethnic Mosaic

More than 50 different ethnic groups live in Ghana, each with its own beliefs, traditions, and language or dialect. Such diversity would seem to make for conflict among the groups, but in Ghana this has not usually been the case. The differences among the Ghanaian people form the fabric of a unified nation—much like threads of different colors form the unique geometrical designs in Ghana's vibrant *kente* cloth.

The Akan are Ghana's largest ethnic group. About 44 percent of Ghana's 18 million people belong to the Akan and its subgroups, such as the Asante, Akyem, Akwapim, Akwamu, Agona, Kwahu, Denkyira, Nzema, Brong, Krobo, and Fante. The Akan-related people live primarily in the southern half of the country, and have had the longest contact with Europeans and Western life-styles. All Akan speak a common language called Twi, but each ethnic subgroup has its own dialect (for example, the Asante speak Asante Twi, and the Fante speak Fante Twi).

Ghana's northern regions are inhabited by the Mossi-Dagomba, Gurma, Guan, Fulani, Frafra, Mamprusi, Gonja, Nanumba, and Wala. These ethnic groups comprise about 30 percent of Ghana's population. Each has its own language, but all speak Hausa, a trading language common to West Africa. Northerners have been less influenced by Western life-styles and have maintained many of their religious and cultural traditions.

Two other major ethnic groups are the Ewe and the Ga-Adangme. The Ewe, who make up 13 percent of the population, live in the Volta region along Ghana's eastern border and speak Ewe. The Ga-Adangme inhabit the coastal region around Accra; they make up about 8 percent of Ghana's population and speak Ga.

English is Ghana's official language. At independence the government decided that English was the best choice for a national language because it was not identified with any ethnic group. However, the government has made five languages, including Hausa, "semiofficial" languages in which it conducts government business.

Religions

The principal religions practiced in Ghana are Christianity, Islam, and traditional African religions. About 24 percent of Ghana's people are Christians. Christianity was brought to the country in the late 15th century when Portuguese priests accompanying trading ships landed on the Gold Coast and converted many of the coastal peoples to Catholicism. In the 1800s, Protestant missionaries came to the Gold Coast and established churches and schools throughout southern Ghana. Today, most Christians are found in the southern part of the country.

The people of northern Ghana are chiefly Muslim (followers of Islam). Arab traders transporting gold north to the Sudan introduced Islam into Ghana around the 17th century. Muslim Ghanaians make up about 30 percent of the country's population.

About 38 percent of Ghana's people practice traditional African religions. Many of these traditional religions are polytheistic (involving the worship of many gods or spirits). These lesser gods are under the ultimate control of a supreme being or god who is called

"Onyame" or "Onyankopon" by the Akan and "Mawu" by the Ewes.

Followers of traditional religions believe that spirits live on the earth in various natural objects such as trees, lakes, mountains, or plants. Some inhabit shrines or figures called fetishes, from the Portuguese word *feticio,* which means "charm." Each ethnic group has its own gods and fetishes. A shrine fetish may be built in the center of a village and become the site for ceremonial offerings, such as the blood of a chicken.

An offering like this is believed to appease the gods. However, the gods can also be angered. A bad harvest may be blamed on a god

This Muslim in northern Ghana relaxes in a cultivated field most likely tilled with an ox-drawn plow.

who was insulted by a farmer. To guard against illness or disaster, a Ghanaian may wear a talisman, an object believed to have special powers that is worn on the body.

The priesthood plays an important role in traditional religions. A priest or priestess will become possessed by a particular spirit and offer guidance on matters such as marriage, farming, curing illness, or settling disputes. Members of the priesthood are respected members of a village, and are regularly consulted.

Occupations

About 64 percent of Ghana's people live in rural areas and work as farmers. Ghanaians who own large palm-oil and cacao plantations,

A fetish dancer has thrown himself into a trance.

A young Ghanaian woman sells her wares at Makola marketplace in Accra.

or who cultivate large farms, are wealthy. Most Ghanaians, however, earn meager livings farming one or two acres of land. They grow enough food to feed their families and, in good years, have a surplus left over to take to the market.

In the large central markets of Accra and Kumasi, women control the food trade and are a potent force in the country's economy. These market women sell baskets of produce as well as household goods and cotton print cloth. Market women often have large families to support, and are likely to contribute more income to the household than their husbands.

A small professional class exists in Ghana's urban centers. Many of these lawyers, doctors, nurses, teachers, business professionals, and civil servants have been educated in the universities of Europe and the United States. Other urban Ghanaians work in offices as clerks, secretaries, and managers. Ghana's cities also have a large force of factory workers.

In recent years many Ghanaians have left the countryside for the cities in search of jobs with higher wages. Unfortunately, few jobs have been available and many of these job seekers remain unemployed. The available jobs are mainly low-paying positions, such as domestic servants or night-soil (human waste) collectors. Many who have made the trek to the city finally decide to return to their rural villages.

Life-styles

As in any society, a Ghanaian's life-style depends on his or her income level. Ghana's wealthiest citizens can afford large modern houses with hot and cold water, air conditioning, a telephone, and television. Most of the private cars in Ghana are owned by the wealthy. Ghana's poorest citizens are subsistence farmers (farmers who grow only enough to eat) who live in remote rural villages. Their homes are made of earthen walls and thatched roofs and do not have basic utilities such as electricity and indoor plumbing.

Many Ghanaians live between these two extremes in compounds that house members of the immediate and extended family. A typical house in the villages of southern Ghana is built of wood and plaster or earthen bricks in a rectangular shape with a thatch or tin roof. The rooms center around an interior courtyard. Sheep, goats, dogs, chickens, pigs, and other livestock are kept in and around the compound in stalls.

In the north, traditional houses are in a cylindrical shape. The walls are made of a mixture of cow dung and earth, and the conical roofs are made of thatch. Several cylindrical rooms may be joined with a wall to form an inner courtyard. Grain is stored in similar-shaped granaries around the compound.

On a visit to a Ghanaian family's compound, one will always find the women of the house preparing the day's meals. Ghanaians take great pride in their traditional dishes. One of the most popular is *fufu,* a mixture of cassava or yams and plantain (a type of banana) that is boiled and then pounded into a sticky dumpling. The fufu is served with thick, red palm-oil soup or peanut stew, laden with pieces of fish or chicken and vegetables.

A staple in the diets of all Ghanaians is corn, which may be roasted or boiled on the cob. Corn kernels are also milled into flour and made into *kenkey* and *banku* dumplings. *Kontumire,* a leafy green vegetable similar to spinach, is another popular food. It is mixed with palm oil to make a stew that is served with slices of ripe, sweet, boiled plantain.

Fish is an important source of protein in the Ghanaian diet. To prevent spoilage, fish is sun-dried, smoked, or salted. Ghanaians also eat fowl, goats, sheep, and cattle.

Alcoholic beverages are usually prepared from locally grown grains. *Pito,* which tastes something like beer, is brewed from millet. Palm wine is tapped directly from the tree and is naturally fermented. The wine is also distilled to make *akpeteshie,* a potent, pure-grain alcohol.

Festivals and Holidays

Festivals are held to celebrate harvests and the new year, and to remember ancestors. Each ethnic group has its own unique festivals. The Akan remember the dead with several small festivals that lead up to a large celebration at the end of the year. The Akan have their own calendar, which divides the year into nine cycles of 40 days each. Each 40-day period, or *adae* (a Twi word meaning resting place), ends with a special day of worship when the Akan chief and his elders call on the spirits of departed chiefs.

These chiefs' spirits are represented by sacred stools, hand-carved seats that symbolize a chief's throne and spirit. The Akan's sacred stools are kept in a special room that can be entered by the chief and the elders of the group only on the day of the adae's end. The chief and the elders bring water and specially prepared food to offer to the spirits, and they ask the spirits for guidance in ruling the Akan. Court musicians play drums until dusk, when the adae rituals end.

A ceremonial stools have played an important part in the history and tradition of Ghana.

Most Akan mark the final adae cycle—and the beginning of the new year—with Odwira, a week-long festival that is usually held in October. Noisemaking, singing, drumming, and dancing are banned for 40 days prior to the festival. A parade or a feast takes place every day in the Odwira week. On the last day of the festival, all the chiefs in the region gather for a day-long celebration called the Durbar. Dressed in their finery, the chiefs stand beneath large, richly colored umbrellas and listen to speeches honoring them. Drumming, dancing, and feasting continue into the evening.

Other ethnic groups celebrate similar festivals. In August, the Ga celebrate the corn harvest with Homowo. The Ewe hold several different festivals to observe the yam harvest. Ghana's northern ethnic groups, such as the Dagomba, Mamprusi, Gonja, Nanumba, and Wala, celebrate Damba, an Islamic festival honoring the birth of the prophet Mohammed.

Ghana's state holidays include Independence Day (March 6), which marks the day the country broke free of British colonial rule in 1957. June 4 marks the day in 1979 that Ghana's present leader, Flight Lieutenant Jerry Rawlings, was released from prison after a failed coup (takeover of the government) attempt. Another holiday is December 31, the day Rawlings returned to power in 1981. Both holidays feature military processions and speeches about the nation's future.

Cape Coast Castle sits above the harbor on the Gulf of Guinea, where local fishermen anchor fishing pirogues, which are often constructed from a single tree trunk.

The History of Ghana

Modern Ghana is named after the ancient West African kingdom of Ghana. Ancient Ghana was located south of the Sahara Desert in a geographical region known as the Western Sudan. (Today, the region is the location of the nations of Senegal, Mali, Niger, Burkina Faso, Mauritania, Guinea, and Nigeria). The first inhabitants of the Western Sudan migrated to the region from the eastern part of Africa about 50,000 years ago. These early inhabitants moved into the savanna and grasslands and survived by hunting animals and gathering edible wild plants.

By 10,000 B.C., these hunter-gatherers had migrated from the kingdom of Ghana into what is now modern Ghana. Archaelogists have found stone tools on the plains outside Accra that date back to the late Stone Age (5500–2500 B.C.), indicating that hunter-gatherers had reached the Atlantic Ocean at that time. Because of their nomadic way of life, these early inhabitants did not build permanent settlements in Ghana.

In the 5th century A.D., Arab merchants forged trade routes from North Africa into the Western Sudan in their search for gold and ivory. These merchants made contact with several tribal communities that had developed agricultural societies in the region. The

Arabs traded salt for the gold of the Sudanic peoples; the salt was then used to preserve fish and beef.

Between the 9th and 11th centuries, the ancient kingdom of Ghana became the most important trading center in the Western Sudan. The kingdom grew wealthy from its control of the goldfields in the region. In the 14th century, the Mali Empire overthrew the kingdom of Ghana. The Malis opened new gold mines in what is now modern Ghana, and the first permanent settlers moved into Ghana.

According to Ghanaian legends, these settlers were the ancestors of modern Ghanaians such as the Akan. These early settlers expanded the trade route used by the Arabs by forming their own trading states. Bono-Mansu and Banda were two of the earliest known states within the boundaries of modern Ghana.

Europeans came to the area during the 15th century. Portuguese traders in search of gold were the first to appear. They arrived

in 1470 and called the coastal region "Mina de Ouro" (Gold Mine). To protect the lucrative trade from other Europeans, the Portuguese built a fort on the Mina de Ouro in 1482.

According to legend, a local chief named Caramanca told the Portuguese that building the fort would harm the peaceful relations between the Europeans and his people. When the Portuguese began building the fort, Caramanca's people attacked the Portuguese for disturbing a sacred place. However, Caramanca and the Portuguese reached an agreement; the Portuguese could construct their fort if they promised to stay out of local affairs and pay rent for the use of the land.

Elmina Castle—the name of the completed fort—became the headquarters for Portuguese trade in Africa throughout the 16th century. The Portuguese built other forts at the mouths of the An-kobra and Pra rivers, but they did not try to impose Portuguese rule

On the beach of Elmina, slaves were loaded into boats for the transfer to larger, ocean-going vessels.

on the people living around the forts. Local chiefs were left to govern their tribes, but the tribes living near the forts sometimes looked to the Portuguese for protection from enemy tribes.

Britain and France made their first trading voyages to the Gold Coast in the mid-16th century, but they did not challenge Portugal's claim to the coast. The Dutch did challenge the Portuguese, however, when Dutch ships reached the Gold Coast in 1597 and attacked the Portuguese fort at Axim. The Dutch were driven off, but they managed to gain a foothold in the Gold Coast trade by establishing relations with the Asebu tribe. In 1612, the Dutch constructed a fort at Mori, east of Elmina. Over the next two decades, the Dutch presence increased, and in 1637 they captured Elmina Castle and other Gold Coast forts from the Portuguese.

By this time, humans had replaced gold as the object of the traders' interest. Europeans looked to Africa for the manpower required to work the plantations in their colonies in the West Indies and America. The traders transformed their forts into auction houses and temporary prisons for slave captives. Many captives died during the long crossing over the Atlantic Ocean, succumbing to disease, starvation, or the cruel punishments inflicted upon them by the ships' captains.

Africans themselves played a key role in the slave trade. Europeans had no knowledge of the African interior and relied on the native Africans to serve as slave suppliers and distributors. African slavers, described by a Dutch trader in the late 17th century as "kings, rich men, and prime merchants," met the European demand for slaves by capturing tribespeople from the interior. Tribal states along the coast came into existence and rose to power on the profits of the slave trade.

The Akan people of the coastal and forest regions, and the Asante people of the central region increased their power and wealth by trading slaves for European goods. European traders often paid the Africans with guns, which helped to fuel tribal rivalries. Tribal groups abandoned other types of trade for the greater wealth to be had from the slave trade. By the early 1700s, "man stealing" had become a profitable occupation among powerful tribal groups. The price paid by British traders for one male captive exceeded the value of three ounces of gold.

During the 18th century, the Asante people became the Gold Coast's major supplier of slaves. They also became a powerful and independent state because of the slave trade. The Asante ruled over other tribal groups until the beginning of the 20th century.

Under a leader named Osei Tutu, the Asante had overthrown the Denkyira tribe in 1701. The Asante used European firearms to conquer the Akyem people in 1742 and seized control of the region's gold mines. The Asante also conquered the savanna states farther north, which were occupied by non-Akan tribes such as the Dagomba and the Gonja. By the mid-18th century, much of the middle and upper Gold Coast fell under the sovereignty of the Asante.

The End of Slavery

In the early 1800s, the movement to abolish the slave trade spread throughout Europe. Denmark outlawed slave trading in 1802, as did Great Britain in 1807. Within a decade, the Netherlands and France had also abandoned the slave trade. However, slave labor continued on the British plantations of the West Indies until 1833 and in the United States until after the Civil War.

The Asante Empire reached the height of its power during the early 1800s. The Asante nation stretched from the traditional Gonja tribal area in the north toward the coast. Tribes under Asante rule were allowed limited independence, but some rebelled and became allies of the Fante tribe, which controlled the coast.

The Asante and the Fante battled throughout the 1800s. Asante invasions of Fante territory often involved Europeans. The Dutch

maintained good relations with the Asante, while the British supported the Fante. In 1816, the Dutch governor sent an ambassador to the Asante capital of Kumasi to negotiate the construction of a Dutch-built highway that would link Elmina with Kumasi. The British feared that the highway would give the Dutch control of the Gold Coast trade, so they sent their own representative to Kumasi to improve relations with the Asante. Both the Dutch and the British signed a treaty with the tribe.

In 1823, British trade on the Gold Coast fell under the jurisdiction of the British governor in Sierra Leone, who did not honor the treaty's terms. Asante soldiers killed the British governor in an

The Cape Coast Castle is situated on a rocky promontory. This is a view of the outer fortress.

ambush. This encounter with the British was the first of several that led to the eventual downfall of the Asante kingdom.

In 1830, the British government sent Captain George Maclean to administer the Gold Coast trade. Maclean's administration lasted until 1842 and laid the foundation for British control of the Gold Coast. Maclean tripled exports from the coast, making the production of palm oil the leading industry. He also helped foster a peace treaty between the Asante and other coastal tribes and helped settle local tribal disputes.

The Danish left the Gold Coast in 1850, selling their forts and other properties to the British. In 1872, the British reached a similar agreement with the Dutch. The departure of the Dutch left Great Britain as the sole European power on the Gold Coast.

The coastal forts now served as British military and naval bases and protected British interests from the Asante, who attacked the British seven times between 1811 and 1874. When the British took over Elmina Castle, a large group of Asante marched to the coast to claim Elmina as their own. Their allies living in a village outside the fort joined the invaders; the British retaliated and burned the village to the ground. This battle immediately led to the Sagrenti War of 1874, and to the British destruction of the Asante capital at Kumasi.

The British forced the Asante to sign the Treaty of Komena, which called for the surrender of the Asante's Gold Coast states south of the Pra and Ofin rivers. This area was then made a British colony in 1874. The British also demanded that the Asante keep trade routes on the Gold Coast open and pay a large fine in gold.

In 1884, the major European powers gathered in Berlin to divide African lands below the Sahara Desert among themselves. Great Britain and France obtained most of the colonies, with the remaining few going to Portugal, Belgium, and Germany. Great Britain kept the area agreed to in the Treaty of Komena. Britain also wanted to control the northern territories of the Gold Coast as protection against the increasing influence of the German colony of Togoland to the east and the French colony of the Ivory Coast to the west.

In 1896, the British attempted to establish a political base in Kumasi. Fearing that the British would try to make the remainder of their kingdom part of the Gold Coast colony, the Asante sent a delegation to London to ask Queen Victoria for the Asante's independence. The British ignored the Asante's plea and sent soldiers to Kumasi. They imprisoned the Asantahene (king), Prempeh I, and exiled him to the Seychelles Island, off the coast of East Africa.

The British constructed a large military fort in Kumasi and maintained control over the Asante. But in 1900, the British colonial governor visited Kumasi and demanded that the Asante surrender the Golden Stool—the symbol of the Asante kingship and religious authority—to the British crown. The governor even requested that he be allowed to sit on the Golden Stool, which the Asante king was forbidden to do.

The Asante revolted at this attempt at domination. For eight months, they relentlessly attacked the British fort at Kumasi. The governor fled Kumasi and returned to Accra. Finally, however, British troops sent from Accra defeated the Asante, and the leaders of the Asante revolt joined Prempeh I in exile. The Asante surrendered to the British Gold Coast colony in 1901.

Kwame Nkrumah was Ghana's first prime minister after the nation received independence in 1957.

Moving Toward Independence

The Europeans expected their African colonies to be profitable. In this respect, the Gold Coast was a model for the other colonies. Small farms grew crops such as beans, corn, peanuts, tomatoes, onions, and eggplant. Large plantations produced profitable export items, such as palm oil and cocoa. The former territory of the Asante provided most of the colony's wealth with its cocoa and timber industries and its gold and diamond mines. European firms controlled many of these resources.

The British collected money through import-export taxes, the leasing and sale of land, and the sale of mineral rights. But the Gold Coast's largest source of income came from the plantations. Africans provided cheap and plentiful labor, and their meager wages were heavily taxed by the colonial government. In effect, the African people served as "wage slaves" in their own land.

Many Africans criticized Britain's colonial administration. They wanted to govern themselves, and they protested British rules that kept Africans out of top government positions. In 1920, a group of Gold Coast Africans formed the National Congress of British West Africa (NCBWA) and demanded political reforms. The NCBWA wanted African representatives elected by the people to serve in the governments of Britain's West African colonies of the Gold Coast, Nigeria, and Sierra Leone. The British paid little attention to the demands of the NCBWA, and the organization folded within a few years. But the movement toward African independence had begun.

The colonial administration did make some superficial changes. In 1925, it created the Provisional Council of Chiefs to encourage cooperation between the colonial administration and traditional rulers. Under a system of government known as indirect rule, the tribal chiefs retained their authority over local matters, while the British remained in control of the colony's national affairs. In truth, the chiefs' limited authority did not affect British power over the people of the Gold Coast.

By the time World War II broke out in 1939, speaking out against British rule had become widespread among the Gold Coast's educated African community. But it was the war that gave the people of the Gold Coast a new sense of solidarity and nationhood. Gold Coast soldiers fought alongside British troops in foreign lands and returned home at the war's end with a new understanding of their colony's place in the world. Moreover, the war had cost the British thousands of lives and enormous sums of money. The Gold Coast people took advantage of Britain's troubled situation after the war to assert their desire for independence.

In 1947, the United Gold Coast Convention (UGCC) was formed to direct the independence movement. The UGCC wanted to replace British rule with an independent government run by Africans. The group's leader, J. B. Danquah, favored gradual reforms that would eventually lead to independence. But the UGCC's outspoken secretary general, Kwame Nkrumah, called for more immediate change. In 1949, Nkrumah, who had studied in the United States and in Great Britain, broke away from the UGCC to form the Convention People's party (CPP). He condemned colonial government and captured Africans' aspirations with the slogan "Self-Government Now."

In 1950, the colonial administration banned the CPP's news-paper and jailed Nkrumah after the CPP staged strikes to protest British rule. The following year, however, the British gave in to mounting pressure and permitted elections of an all-African legis-lature for local affairs. The CPP won a majority of seats, and Nkru-mah was released from jail and allowed to serve in the legislature.

After CPP victories in the 1954 and 1956 legislative elections, Nkrumah pushed for complete independence from British rule. On March 6, 1957, amid joyful celebration, the Gold Coast became the first African colony to become independent. The country was re-named "Ghana" and Nkrumah became its prime minister. Ghana inspired a wave of independence movements in other African colo-nies. Within a few years, many other new nations began to emerge from European colonialism in Africa.

After Independence

At independence, the Ghanaian people had high hopes for their new country. Nkrumah intended to make Ghana the most modern nation

Jerry Rawlings, who first came to power in 1979, established national holidays to commemorate crucial dates in his public career.

on the African continent. With the help of foreign investors, the CPP government built factories, roads, schools and universities, and hospitals. A new harbor was built at Tema. The most ambitious project was the completion of a hydroelectric dam on the Volta River, which provided electricity for most of the country. The government also established Ghana Airways and enlarged Accra's airport to handle international air traffic.

Ghana adopted a new constitution in 1960, changing from a parliamentary government with a prime minister as head of state to a republican government with a president as head of state. Nkrumah continued as leader. However, the world market for cocoa and other exports from Ghana began to decline. As profits fell, the government had less money to spend. Prices rose as imported goods became scarce. Ghana borrowed from other nations to support its economy and fell heavily into debt.

Nkrumah spoke of transforming Ghana into a Socialist state in which all industries would be under the government's control. But opposition to his leadership grew as Ghana's economy worsened. Nkrumah jailed his opponents and censored the press to maintain authority. His ties with the Soviet Union angered Great Britain and the United States, who had given Ghana loans and invested in its industries.

Nkrumah's administration fell on February 24, 1966, when his police and military forces staged a coup (the sudden and usually violent overthrow of a government). Nkrumah went into exile in Guinea, where he lived until his death in 1972.

The National Liberation Council (NLC) replaced Nkrumah's government. General Joseph Akrah and other military officers headed the NLC. The United States recognized the new regime and sent financial aid to bolster Ghana's economy.

A parade of "young pioneers" marks the anniversary of the attempted assassination of Nkrumah.

The NLC lifted Nkrumah's ban on political parties and called for elections in 1969. The Progress party, led by Kori Busia, won a majority of seats in the Legislative Assembly. Busia became prime minister, while the presidency went to Edward Akufo-Addo. However, the new government was unable to repair Ghana's ailing economy; cocoa prices continued to drop and foreign debt increased.

On January 13, 1972, the army acted again and overthrew Akufo-Addo's government. Colonel Ignatius Kutu Acheampong installed the National Redemption Council as Ghana's ruling government, suspended the constitution, and banned political parties.

Ghana's economy continued to get worse. On July 5, 1978, the army quietly removed Acheampong from office and replaced him with Lieutenant General Frederick Akuffo. Convinced that a civilian government would do a better job of running the country, Akuffo scheduled elections for June 1979. But as the economy continued its downward spiral of high prices, depressed wages, and food shortages, another military faction decided to take action.

On May 15, 1979, Flight Lieutenant Jerry Rawlings, an officer in Ghana's air force, tried to overthrow Akuffo. The coup failed. Rawlings was imprisoned to await trial and, most likely, execution. On June 4, 1979, the day of his trial, Rawlings was permitted to broadcast a speech over Ghana's radio station. Rawlings appealed to Ghana's people to unite to save their country and their economy.

The speech won the support of the people and the army. Rawlings was freed from jail the following day. He seized power in a successful coup and installed the Armed Forces Revolutionary Council (AFRC) as Ghana's governing body. He also ordered the execution of Acheampong, Akuffo, and six other high-ranking military officers for corruption and other crimes against the state.

Rawlings said the AFRC would be a temporary government and, true to his word, he permitted free elections to take place in June and July. Hilla Limann was sworn in as president on September 24, 1979. The Limann government adopted a constitution modeled on American and British political principles. But the Ghanaian people soon lost faith in Limann because his government could not stop widespread corruption and rising prices.

Rawlings was critical of the civilian government's inability to control the economy. On December 31, 1981, he overthrew the Limann government. Reasserting his leadership, Rawlings suspended the 1979 constitution, dismissed the president and his cabinet, dissolved the Parliament, and established the Provisional National Defense Council (PNDC) as the ruling body.

Rawlings said he would wage a "holy war" against the corruption he believed was hobbling Ghana's political and economic growth. But although many people had welcomed his first coup, Rawlings's second military government did not receive the same response. Small groups within the army attempted four coups against the PNDC during its first 22 months in power.

In 1992, Rawlings and the PNDC, after creating commissions of inquiry in Ghana's 10 administrative areas, introduced a new constitution establishing universal suffrage and parliamentary democracy. The constitution was approved overwhelmingly by referendum in April 1992, and Rawlings won election in November as president of the Fourth Republic, though his victory was tainted by a boycott of parliamentary elections by major opposition parties.

Nonetheless, Rawlings was reelected in 1996 and his party won a clear majority in parliament in what most Ghanaian and foreign observers said was a fair election with enthusiastic voter turnout. Under the constitution, Rawlings will not be allowed a third term and is scheduled to step down in the year 2000.

Ghana's chief of state, Jerry Rawlings, tours the Chicago exchange with its president. Rawlings is there to promote western business investment in Ghana.

Government
and Economy

Jerry Rawlings's several turns as Ghana's head of state, both as leader of military coups and as elected president, have suggested a man who holds a consistent view of his country's future. For years his public statements in support of democratic rule were dismissed as mere rhetoric by his opponents within Ghana. In light of the recent elections, however, his long-delayed promises of democracy appear to have been genuine.

His government has shown continued, strong support for education, the advancement of women, the rooting out of government corruption, and the welfare of the poorer citizens. He has also undertaken many economic reforms, such as privatizing state-owned industries and improving fiscal management. These reforms have drawn international investors and loans to Ghana. Budget deficits, however, present an ongoing problem, and the overall standard of living in Ghana has increased only slowly.

Under Rawlings, the country has weathered such severe strains to the nation as the forced return of a million Ghanaians from Nigeria in 1983, two major droughts, and the general upheaval resulting from the civil war in Liberia during the early 1990s. The Liberian situation not only brought a flood of refugees to Ghana but also involved the entire West African community in Liberian affairs through efforts to stop the fighting and to establish the basis for a stable Liberian government.

Ghana's 1992 constitution divides powers among the president, the parliament, a cabinet appointed by the president and approved by parliament, a Council of State, and an independent judiciary. Many of the mechanisms set in place by the Provisional National Defense Council (PNDC) to increase local representation have been expanded and liberalized under the 1992 constitution. For example, the PNDC established councils in each of Ghana's 10 administrative regions to introduce a degree of local control, though the central government appointed the council leaders. This type of local control has increased under the democratic government, with assemblies established in each of the 110 districts that together form the 10 administrative regions. The regions now also elect representatives to the national parliament.

The government has developed closer ties with the tribal chiefs, Ghana's traditional rulers. Although many of their responsibilities are now ceremonial, the chiefs have a special role among their people that the national government cannot ignore. The traditional chiefs have jurisdiction over matters such as land distribution and ownership, petty theft, and family quarrels.

The Asantahene (the traditional king) is the most powerful chief in Ghana. At first, he and other tribal chiefs opposed the PNDC's programs, but Rawlings met with the Asantahene in 1984 and received the chief's pledge that he would cooperate with the government.

Rawlings came to power as a populist leader, one who wanted the government to serve the interests of the "common man": the workers, farmers, and fishermen. However, he lost the support of many workers by cutting back on government funding of social services such as health care and by supporting cuts in workers' wages.

His attempts to impose a value-added tax in 1995 led to strikes and massive social unrest, and he was forced to withdraw the tax.

His continuing promises to restore democracy to the country by holding local and national elections went unfulfilled for years. Civil liberties were suspended for over a decade, and the PNDC maintained total censorship of the news media. Many in Ghana feared that Rawlings merely wished to hold onto power, as was true of many African leaders of the time.

However, opposition movements demanding the restoration of democracy grew, and in 1992 Rawlings introduced the current constitution, one of the most progressively democratic documents in any African nation. The major question remaining is the direction Ghana will take when Rawlings's second term expires.

The Economic Recovery Program

When Rawlings took control in 1981, he said Ghana's economy was a "runaway train" headed straight for disaster. Inflation was more than 100 percent and the price paid for cocoa, Ghana's main

The cocoa tree is the most important foreign exchange earner for Ghana's economy.

export, was at its lowest level in ten years. In 1983, after several unsuccessful attempts at reversing Ghana's economic decline, the government started an Economic Recovery Program (ERP). The ERP has led to a decrease in prices and the first real growth in the country's gross domestic product in years.

The ERP was originally intended to help agricultural production, especially the production of export crops such as cocoa. Soon after Ghana gained independence, the price for cocoa on the world market suddenly dropped. Prices for other raw materials and resources produced in Africa fell as well. As a result of the drop in prices, Ghana's earnings dropped. The government, as the sole buyer of export crops, was forced to pay farmers for their surplus crops. Because the farmers were earning less than it cost them to grow export crops, they planted less. Harvests shrank and Ghana's economy began a rapid decline.

More than half of Ghana's work force is employed in agriculture. Many are subsistence farmers who grow just enough food to feed their families. When Ghana's export crop farmers began planting less, some subsistence farmers became discouraged and planted less. Food became scarce and food prices rose, although wages did not.

The ERP was designed to solve these problems. Formulated by Finance and Economic Planning Minister Kwesi Botchwey, the program was introduced in 1983. But a devastating drought that had begun in 1982 continued until 1984, hindering the progress of the new economic plan.

Another major drag on the economy was the return in 1983 of one million Ghanaians who were expelled from Nigeria. Many Ghanaians had left the country in the preceding decade to find work. Many went to Nigeria, where high-paying jobs were plentiful because of Nigeria's oil boom. But the world price for oil dropped suddenly and Nigeria's economy slumped. The Nigerian government ordered all foreign workers to leave the country immediately. The million

(continued on page 65)

SCENES OF
GHANA

◄ Mampong Scarf is the country's main source of gold, one of Ghana's most valuable exports.

➤ Linguists with decorated golden staffs are the chief spokespersons of the chiefs.

∇ A traffic policeman in British-style uniform directs traffic in Accra.

◄ *A young Ghanaian displays her native costume.*

▲ *Fresh produce and all sorts of goods are sold by hundreds of vendors in Makola market in Accra.*

▼ *These men at a ceremony display the wide variety of dress among Ghanaians.*

➤ *One of Ghana's main exports is cocoa.*
These beans are being sun-dried.

❯ *Villagers wash clothes at sunset in a lake near Tamale in northern Ghana.*

▼ *Nana Opoku Ware II, the Asantahene, sits in state next to the Golden Stool. The stool is the symbol of Asante kingship.*

↑ *A Ghanaian woman rests among her wares at market.*

➤ *Termite mounds, such as these in northern Ghana, reach heights of up to seven feet. They are constructed by the termites to bring air to the colony, which lies below ground.*

➤ *This gold headpiece is from the Asantahene's court in Kumasi.*

⋏ *Along Ghana's Atlantic coastline, the tropical vegetation is lush and the surf is heavy.*

➤ *This Kente cloth is made of silk and cotton.*

Ghanaians who returned home found the Ghanaian economy in shambles.

By the end of 1984, the drought had subsided. Most Ghanaian farmers reaped large harvests in the following planting season. The cocoa harvest, however, was extremely poor because Ghana had lost almost one-third of its cocoa crop to brush fires that had raged during the drought.

In recent years, Ghana's economy has improved. Cocoa prices have gone up, and the ERP has had some effect. The World Bank and the International Monetary Fund, two of the most important sources of funds for Third World countries, also came to Ghana's aid. They pledged close to $600 million in loans to Ghana, on the condition that the government spend the money on development projects and reduce the government's budget deficit and inflation rate.

Some of the loan money has been used to replant cocoa farms and increase the production of export crops. Other money has been invested in Ghana's timber industry. Ghana's rain forests contain very valuable species of trees, such as teak and mahogany. Yet timber production, which was Ghana's second largest export, had declined after years of neglect. Since the government has modernized Ghana's timber mills, production has increased.

Other industries are also being improved. Factories built during Nkrumah's regime are receiving new machinery. The government is trying to attract foreign investors to Ghana while also encouraging local industries such as textile manufacturers, canneries, and food-processing plants. Rawlings's government has been particularly committed to rebuilding the country's export trade, and by 1993 the total value of Ghana's annual exports reached $1 billion, led by shipments of cocoa, gold, timber, and tuna.

One of the most important steps toward Ghana's economic recovery has been the government's devaluation of its currency, the *cedi*. The cedi was introduced in 1965 to replace the West African pound. The exchange rate (official worth) of one cedi was set at one U.S. dollar. As Ghana's economy began to falter, however, the real value of the cedi also dropped, so that by 1983 one cedi was worth only a few U.S. cents.

Soon the difference between the official value of the cedi and its actual purchasing power was so great that banks in other countries refused to honor Ghana's money. The government, however, refused to recognize the problem and adjusted the cedi's value only slightly. The black market (an illegal or unofficial money exchange) gave Ghanaians the means to exchange their cedis for other currencies at a rate many times lower than the cedi's official value. In 1981, U.S. $10 would "buy" 600 cedis on the black market, but a Ghanaian bank would give less than 30 cedis for U.S. $10.

Because so much of Ghana's food had to be imported and paid for in foreign currencies, food prices for Ghanaians were very high. For example, in 1981 one pound of rice cost the equivalent of more

Workmen pour molten aluminum into steel molds at the Volta Aluminum Co. Ltd. plant in Tema.

than U.S. $40 at the official exchange rate. At the cedi's black-market rate, however, the price for the same amount of rice was $3 or $4. But black-market prices were affordable only to those who had access to foreign currency. The government fixed the prices of staple commodities such as corn, rice, flour, meat, and fish, to try to keep food costs down. But most Ghanaians, however, found even basic foods expensive.

The decision to devalue (lower) the cedi's official rate helped bring the currency in line with reality. More significantly, starting with the economic reforms of 1983, Rawlings's government began to turn away from a socialist model of state ownership and close control of production, distribution, prices, and other aspects of the economy. In recent years, hundreds of state-owned industries have been sold to private, competitive companies, and foreign investment has been successfully encouraged.

Under the economic reforms, Ghana is at last putting its natural resources to better use. From the late 1980s through the mid-1990s, the economy showed a 5 percent growth rate and a per capita output double that of its poorer West African neighbors. By the late 1990s, the total gross domestic product was roughly $8 billion, and exports were still increasing.

On the negative side, subsistence agriculture still accounts for almost half of the gross domestic product, employing some 55 percent of the work force. Unemployment hovers around 10 percent of the work force, and the country's deficit continues to increase. It will take many years of hard work and careful economic planning to ensure all Ghanaians a job, decent wages, and a stable economy.

Classrooms at Nkrumah University at Kumasi are well appointed. The country has three universities, and students compete vigorously for admission.

Education
and Health

"Education is the firmest foundation of all for any nation-building process," proclaimed Ghana's first president, Kwame Nkrumah. Nkrumah wanted all Ghanaians to have the opportunity to receive an education equal to that available in Europe or the United States. His legacy of education lives on today, with Ghana's current government contributing the largest percentage of its budget to education of any West African nation.

Primary and junior school education is free for all Ghanaian children, except for textbook fees. A child usually starts primary school at age six. A typical primary school has six forms, or grades. Each form takes one school year to complete. During the first two forms, students are instructed in one of Ghana's major languages, such as Twi, Fante, Ewe, or Ga. From the third form on, Ghanaian students are taught in English, Ghana's official language, and must learn to read and write English. Many children already know some English or can speak it fluently by the time they begin school.

Before educational reforms were instituted in the 1980s, students moved from primary school to four years of middle school, from which they could go, by passing a very difficult examination, to a secondary (high) school. The secondary schools, usually boarding schools where students lived on campus and returned home for vacations, provided seven years of academic studies to prepare students for one of Ghana's three universities or for a technical school.

The Rawlings government felt that this preparation period was too long and too heavily focused on academic subjects, discouraging many students from going on to university education. In the mid-1980s, the government introduced the three-year junior secondary school (JSS), which replaced both the middle school and the first three years of secondary school. Students who plan to go on to a university now advance from the JSS to three years of senior secondary school (SSS).

Besides reducing the number of years of education, the reforms also shifted the JSS and SSS focus from strictly academic studies to one of technical and vocational skills, which the government felt would be more useful and relevant to the country's economic needs. These changes met with strong resistance across the country, and initial examination results from the JSS system indicated little educational success. However, the government has retained the JSS system despite protests.

Other major goals of the educational reform movement have been to increase literacy, to increase the quality of women's education, and to encourage more women to stay in school. To date, the attempts to improve women's education have borne little fruit.

In higher education, the government is working to build a new university and to upgrade two specialized colleges to university level, which would greatly increase the number of students who could be admitted. Some Ghanaian students continue their education in Europe and the United States, and the government assists many of them with scholarships for study abroad.

By the 1990s, the government's expenditure on education had increased to more than a quarter of the country's total annual budget. The government felt that this amount was out of balance and decided that students should pay some of the costs of their education. Despite these new charges, shortages of books and supplies plague the primary and JSS schools. Teachers' salaries cannot keep pace with the increasing cost of living, forcing many teachers to seek other occupations.

The government has also found it increasingly difficult to administer boarding schools, which provide food and housing to students. The tuition-free universities also suffer from decreasing government funds and teacher shortages. Intense student protests, especially in 1993, accompanied the government's decision to begin charging room and board (formerly free) to university students.

Health Care

Modern cities and big hospitals are often out of reach for the nearly two-thirds of Ghanaians who live in rural areas. Most villages continue to rely on local healers, who use traditional treatment methods.

One traditional healer is the village midwife, who delivers babies and treats various health ailments. The midwife may also act as the village pharmacist, giving out basic drugs such as aspirin and chloroquine, which is used to treat malaria, a deadly disease transmitted by mosquitoes.

Another traditional healer is the fetish priest. The fetish priest is believed to have contact with spirits who assist him in healing rituals. As part of a ritual, the priest collects herbs and calls on certain spirits to give them healing properties. The priest then boils the herbs in water to make tea, or crushes them to make a salve for external wounds.

In an attempt to bring together traditional and modern medical practices, the government sponsors a primary health-care program that uses traditional healers to educate Ghanaians about proper health care. The local practitioners teach basic hygiene and explain

Most Ghanaians are animists and often seek to solve their problems with fetish priests or native healers. These men are of the Ewe people.

the connection between unsanitary conditions and disease. Villagers are taught simple health precautions such as boiling drinking water to kill bacteria.

The second level of Ghana's health-care system is a network of rural health clinics run by religious organizations. Doctors and nurses travel to the country's most remote villages to give out medicines and vaccinate rural Ghanaians against disease.

The third level of health care is Ghana's modern hospital system. Ghana has several large hospitals that date from the colonial period. However, the country's economic decline caused shortages of medicines, doctors and nurses, and modern medical equipment. The government has begun to import new medical equipment and has raised doctors' salaries. It has also begun to make medical patients pay some of the costs of their medical care at government-run hospitals.

In the last decade, the government has greatly improved drinking water and sanitation. National medical insurance was introduced in 1989. Primary medical care is now available to 60 percent of the rural population.

However, serious health problems still afflict Ghana, including tropical diseases such as malaria and cerebral spinal meningitis. The country's birth rate, though dropping, remains high at 35 births per 1,000 people, and the infant mortality rate (the number of children who die soon after birth) is also high: 80 out of every 1,000 infants die from disease and malnutrition. Life expectancy has increased, but only to 54 years for men and 58 years for women. Poor pay for health professionals in Ghana has lured many of them to other West African countries, particularly Nigeria.

"The Atumpan Drummer," by a native artist, is an example of contemporary Ghanaian artwork using a traditional subject.

Ghanaian Arts: Reflecting Traditions

Ghana's ethnic traditions are reflected in the country's music, films, literature, and crafts. For example, highlife is a style of music that combines traditional African instruments with contemporary sounds. Electric guitars and keyboards blend with African drums made from wood and animal skins. Trumpets, trombones, and traditional wind instruments add their distinctive notes to highlife melodies.

Most highlife songs are sung in Twi, the language of the Akan people. Some lyrics tell of daily life, while others use proverbs and biblical parables to express Ghanaian beliefs about the world.

Many Ghanaian highlife musicians have become world famous, including George Darko, whose song, "Akoo Te Brofo" (The Parrot Speaks English), became an international hit in 1982. Highlife is frequently played on Ghanaian radio and is the country's favorite dance music.

Ghana's popular culture includes its own film industry, which produces entertainment features, documentaries, and newsreels. The film industry was established in 1948 by the British colonial administration. Following independence, the British film unit was renamed the Ghana Film Industry Corporation (GFIC). In these early years of statehood, the GFIC produced several documentaries and films, including *No Tears for Ananse,* a 1966 film based on the African folktale of a spider (called *ananse* in Twi) who spreads wisdom across the world.

In recent years, Ghanaians have produced films that have been praised by critics. One such movie, *The Road to Kukurantumi,* tells the story of a young Ghanaian's decision to move from his rural village to the capital city of Accra, where he works as a transport driver.

All of Ghana's major cities have at least one movie theater. In addition to films made in Ghana, cinemas also show films from other countries. Kung-fu movies from Japan and the United States and love stories from India are popular with Ghana's young people.

"A Return from the Farm," by a Ghanaian artist of today, shows a husband and wife carrying their produce from the fields.

Ghana's traditional kente cloth, as shown in this sample, is woven of vibrant colors by textile craftsmen. It is worn for ceremonies and special occasions.

Literature

Storytelling is a key part of Ghana's culture. Every ethnic group has its own myths and legends, which are passed down from parents to their children. These myths and legends touch on many subjects, such as how the universe began and stories about the gods. The best known Ghanaian folktales are the Asante *ananse*, or "spider" stories. The hero of these stories is a clever spider called Kwaku Ananse.

One popular *ananse* story tells how Kwaku Ananse asks the sky god to tell him the secrets of the universe. The sky god first demands that Ananse bring him gifts, including a python, a nest of hornets, a leopard, and a fairy. Kings and other important men have tried to gather these gifts before but have failed. Ananse captures the dangerous gifts and brings them to the sky god, who then tells Ananse the story of the universe. It is in this way that man came to know how the universe began.

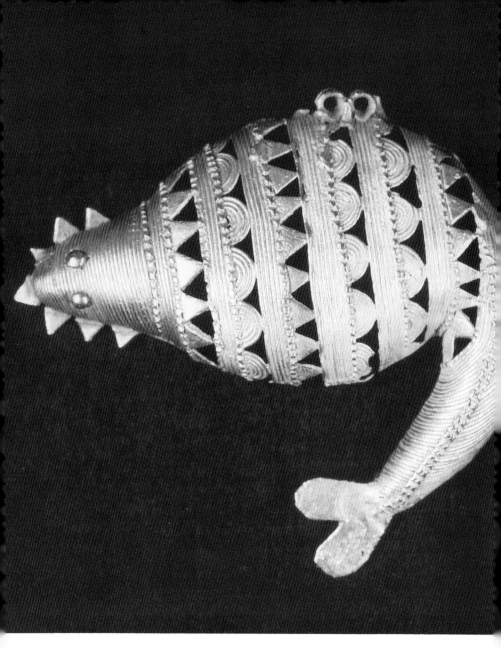

This Ivory Coast hair ornament is made of gold. It reflects the skill and patience of Ghanaian metalworkers.

Storytelling plays a role in traditional ceremonies. Every chief has a linguist who serves as spokesman in all official matters. Among the Akan, the linguist is known as the *okyeame,* or one who communicates to the people the chief's words in poetic terms.

In recent years, Ghana has produced several highly praised works of literature. *The Beautyful Ones Are Not Yet Born,* written in 1969 by Ayi Kwei Armah, is considered a classic. Other Ghanaian novels include *The Breast of the Earth,* by Kofi Awoonor, and *Anowa,* by Christina Ama Ata Aidoo.

Crafts

Sculpture, wood carving, pottery making, metalworking, sandal making, and cloth weaving are some of the crafts at which Ghanaians excel. Many art objects serve religious or ceremonial functions. Kente, a fine, woven cloth, is worn for special occasions such as harvests, weddings, or naming ceremonies. Weavers make the kente cloth on wooden looms, weaving colored threads into long, narrow strips punctuated by geometrical patterns. The colors and designs of the cloth are symbolic of peace, mercy, and wisdom. Adinkra, a cotton cloth stamped with patterns and figures, is worn at funerals.

Painting is a contemporary art form. Young artists often display their works at "galleries" along roads near Ghana's major cities. Since materials are in short supply, artists paint on cloth and wood. Portraiture is especially popular, and the likenesses of famous faces hang in many of the roadside galleries.

The baobab tree, which grows throughout most of Africa, is a common sight in the Ghanaian landscape.

Seeing the Country

Pretend you are a traveler embarking on a journey through Ghana. You will be flying into the capital city of Accra on one of the several international airlines that provide service to Kotoka International, Ghana's major airport. Or perhaps you are flying on a Ghana Airways DC-10, taking advantage of that airline's recently established direct service between New York and Accra.

After checking your bags through customs, you leave the terminal and approach one of the many taxis lined up at the curb. The taxi may perhaps be smaller than you are accustomed to in the United States, but the driver will be no less eager for your business. As you ride away from the airport, you may notice signs of Ghana's recent efforts to promote tourism, such as a Hertz rental car agency or some newly refurbished hotels aimed at attracting the Western traveler.

Accra is a city where traditional African life meets and mingles with modern urban living. Surrounding the city are neighborhoods of both large modern homes and small houses with crude mud walls and tin roofs. As you drive into the center of the city, you notice glass-and-steel highrises towering over crowded streets. Men dressed in business suits and carrying briefcases keep stride with those wearing traditional ankle-length caftans. Women in high heels, flowery summer dresses, and fashionable, elaborately braided hairstyles stroll next to other women wearing the customary African ensemble of sandals, full-length skirts, ruffled tops, and headscarves or wrapped turbans.

Your taxi driver takes you the long way through town, past Danquah Circle, then to Ring Road, which follows the coastline around the city. On the way you pass the Accra Trade Fair building, a futuristic complex with a domed roof where international exhibitions are held to promote Ghanaian products. With the Atlantic Ocean in the background, you pass Christianborg Castle, which has served as Ghana's government headquarters since 1876. The castle is now the official residence of President Rawlings.

Farther up Ring Road is the Accra Arts Council, where Ghanaian dance, theater, and musical groups often perform. Your driver pulls into the lot in front; it is surrounded by wooden kiosks where merchants sell art objects made by Ghanaian craftsmen. Kente cloth, drums, masks, and leather goods are some of the objects that attract your attention on a quick stroll around the lot.

Back on the road, you pass the old Parliament House, where Ghana's first president, Kwame Nkrumah, and other Ghanaian politicians called for Ghana's independence from European rule. The road then passes under the Freedom Arch, an ornately carved stone monolith built in 1957 to celebrate Ghana's newly won independence. The arch stands 55 feet (17 meters) high and 75 feet (23 m) wide.

Across from the Freedom Arch is Black Star Square, an open-air auditorium where Nkrumah delivered many of his speeches. Today, Black Star Square is used for military drills and anniversary celebrations commemorating Ghana's independence and Rawlings's rise to power. The offices of the various government ministries are also located in this part of town.

Traffic slows as you enter Accra's downtown area. This part of Accra resembles a large open-air market. Sidewalk vendors line either side of the street, displaying their goods on tables, in kiosks, or spread out on the ground.

Accra's largest market is Makola Market. The market is actually an open lot crowded with makeshift wooden stalls where women sell basic foodstuffs, spices, clothing, kitchen utensils, charcoal for cooking, and other household goods. Your taxi driver pulls up to the curb to let you have a look around. The market's crowds are as large and colorful as those in the street.

Leaving the center of town, you drive up Independence Avenue, Accra's main thoroughfare. The street reflects the architecture of the colonial era, when wealthy British colonists built magnificent homes with large outdoor verandas, spacious rooms, and sprawling lawns. Many of these houses are now used as foreign embassies, residences for foreign dignitaries, and offices for international organizations such as the United Nations. Accra's international community gives the city a decidedly cosmopolitan, sophisticated air.

Most public meetings, military parades, and major holiday festivals are held in Black Star Square in Accra.

Independence Avenue is also the address of the Ghana Broadcasting Corporation (GBC), the government agency that controls Ghana's radio and television stations. Ghanaians with television sets can watch four channels of GBC-produced programs, including entertainment and drama series and daily news broadcasts. The GBC building has special political significance. In past coup attempts, soldiers struggling to overthrow the government have fought for control of the broadcasting offices, which serve as the only direct link to the Ghanaian people.

Next, you leave Accra to see the rest of the country. Your stops along the coast include the country's two major ports at Takoradi and Tema. The port at Tema, just outside Accra, is equipped to handle many heavy imports such as automobiles and machinery. Imported crude oil is also unloaded here and then processed into gasoline and other oil products at the Tema refinery. Takoradi Harbor handles many of the country's export goods, especially timber.

As you continue your drive along the coast, you will catch a glimpse of coastal village life. Most village residents are fishermen. The fishermen travel far out to sea in *pirogues,* long, narrow canoes made of wood. Each pirogue is given a special name and has an eye painted on the helm. The eye is believed to guide the fishermen safely through rough waters. The fishermen spend several days at sea before returning to shore. When they return, the village women meet the boats and barter with the fishermen for their catch. Some of the fish are sold fresh in the village market. The rest are smoked in round earthen ovens or dried in the sun and then salted. Smoking, drying, and salting prevent spoilage, so the fish can be transported and sold in other markets throughout the country.

Your trip along Ghana's coast would be incomplete without a visit to at least one of the castles and forts built by the Europeans during the Gold Coast slave trade. All but 13 of the 50 strongholds erected along Ghana's coastline are in ruins today. Some, like Chris-

Fishermen launch a boat that is carved from the trunk of a single tree. It is not uncommon for these fishing boats to remain at sea for two to three days.

tianborg Castle in Accra, are used as government facilities. Others are museums where visitors can take guided tours.

Ghana's Interior

As you proceed north from the coast and into the interior, be prepared for a rough ride. Most of Ghana's 25,000 miles (40,000 kilometers) of road are unpaved. You will use Ghana's most frequently traveled and only continuous cross-country road. It extends from Accra to Burkina Faso, a 14-hour drive of some 500 miles (805 kilometers). The journey will take you from the Greater Accra region through the Akwapim Hills of the Eastern region, the forests of the Ashanti region, Brong Ahafo's rolling hills, and the savanna and semidesert of the Northern and Upper regions.

Your first stop outside Accra is Aburi, a small village on the Akwapim ridge. In 1890, the Queen of England established Aburi Gardens, a botanical park that features many exotic species of plants and trees. The gardens overlook the adjoining hills and valleys of

Akwapim and are a popular place for city dwellers to spend the weekend enjoying the peace and beauty of the Ghanaian countryside.

Aburi, just a 45-minute drive north of Accra, is typical of many villages in the southern part of the country. Aburi's 5,000 residents are mostly farmers who grow corn and other staple food crops on small plots of land that may be several miles away from their homes. In Aburi as in Accra, the market is the center of activity. On market day, the village springs to life as people crowd the streets making purchases and haggling over prices.

Your drive continues along the winding road through the lush Akwapim Hills. As you drive farther into Ghana's rural countryside, the villages become smaller. Some consist of only a few mud-walled, thatch-roofed houses clustered together near patches of farmland.

The next major town on your route is Koforidua, where the Ghana Cocoa Research Institute is located. Here, scientists from Ghana and all over the world perform research to improve tropical agriculture.

About halfway between Accra and Kumasi you enter the country's most heavily forested areas. Elephants, leopards, and chimpanzees that once roamed freely in this lush landscape have been driven away by the growing presence of humans. But the forests still abound with monkeys, antelope, bush pigs, civet cats, various species of birds and snakes, and numerous rodents. The skins of some animals command high prices in certain markets.

In the scarp (ridge) ahead of you is gold country. Ghana's largest gold mine is located at Obuasi on the scarp's northern face. Visitors to the Obuasi mine, which lies just south of Kumasi, can see how gold is mined by taking a tour of the mine shaft.

Your next stop is Kumasi in the heart of the Ashanti region. Carved out of the tropical rain forest, Kumasi is a more traditional West African city than Accra—no steel-and-glass highrises loom above this city of 385,000 people. Kumasi is the country's major

The paramount chief of northern Ghana (second from left, in dark robes) makes a state visit to the Asantehene's court in Kumasi.

trading center, and all of Ghana's important exports pass through it. The Ashanti region is Ghana's largest producer of cocoa, gold, and timber.

Kumasi boasts one of the largest open-air marketplaces in West Africa. The Kumasi market covers nearly 2 square miles (5.2 square kilometers) and is crowded with traders and craftsmen displaying every kind of item imaginable. On the market's edges, traders hawk imported goods such as batteries, radios, clothing, watches, and toiletries. Inside the market are long rows of food stands displaying fresh produce, fish and meat, and grains.

Kumasi has many other attractions, including museums that preserve the city's heritage as the center of the ancient Asante kingdom. The Asante are renowned for making kente cloth and for their gold jewelry and traditional gold and bronze ornaments. The National Cultural Center is home to the region's artists and traditional craftsmen, who are highly skilled in weaving, pottery, wood carving, and metalworking.

No visitor to Kumasi should leave without seeing Manhyia Palace, home of the Asante chief. The "palace" is actually a large, modern house on stately grounds. The chief greets his guests in gracious fashion, wearing the traditional kente cloth and splendid Asante gold jewelry. The Asante chief is a world traveler as well. In recent years, he has accompanied the Asante Gold Exhibit to cities throughout Europe and the United States. The exhibit displays some of the finest and most valuable pieces of Asante craftsmanship.

To continue your journey up-country, your taxi driver suggests finding another means of transportation. Most private cars in Ghana are unable to travel the entire 500 miles (805 kilometers) from Accra to the border of Burkina Faso. There are no gas stations outside the major towns, and gasoline is rationed in small quantities to most drivers. Furthermore, the condition of Ghana's main road deteriorates north of Kumasi. Some stretches of road through the hilly, forested region have never been paved and other parts are badly eroded. During the rainy season parts of the road flood. Yet trucks and buses travel daily along this road on long-distance journeys, transporting foodstuffs, cargo, and people from cities to the villages and back again.

Your taxi driver drops you at Kumasi's main lorry park, the region's transportation center. (A lorry is a flat wagon without sides.) Most Ghanaians do not own cars and must rely on public transportation. Any type of road-worthy vehicle with space for more than a driver is considered fit to take passengers. No vehicle leaves the lorry park until every last space is packed full. Ghana's transport vehicles are not always comfortable. Ghanaians often refer to their vehicles as "bone shakers" because passengers often acquire bumps and bruises while traveling over rough roads.

You eventually board a lorry headed for Tamale, the most populous town in Ghana's Northern region. The journey to Tamale takes six hours over very rough sections of road. The forest gives way to the sparsely populated, wide-open expanses of savanna. As you move away from regions dominated by Akan culture into other ethnic communities, villages become smaller and more spread out.

Houses are customarily round and are fitted with conical-shaped roofs made of thatch. The smooth, cylindrical walls of the houses are made from a mixture of the region's red earth and cattle dung. Each family house, or compound, is made up of several cylindrical rooms, arranged in a circle and attached by a wall to create an inner compound for keeping livestock. Smaller cylindrical structures serve as granaries.

Once you reach the lorry park in Tamale, you manage to find a driver who will take you 92 miles (148 kilometers) west over an unpaved road to the Mole Game Reserve, Ghana's only wildlife park. The Mole Game Reserve contains 900 square miles (2,340 square kilometers) of protected land where baboons, monkeys, antelopes, duiker (a smaller relative of the antelope), and elephants freely roam.

Outside the game park is the town of Larabanga, a Gonja village that is the site of one of the oldest mosques in West Africa. The Larabanga mosque has been designated a monument by the villagers and is no longer used for daily prayer. Mosques are a common sight in villages throughout northern Ghana, where most of the people practice Islam.

The remainder of your journey through the upper reaches of Ghana takes you along unpaved, infrequently traveled roads. The way of life there has remained unchanged for centuries. Knotted thorn trees, gnarled, massive baobab trees, and scrub brush cover long stretches of uninhabited savanna. Interrupting the desolation is an occasional dwelling whose inhabitants farm the surrounding fields.

Before winding up your trip through Ghana, you make a last stop in the south at the Akosombo hydroelectric dam in the Volta Region, a thin sliver of land along Ghana's eastern border. The dam

The Akosomba hydroelectric dam in the Volta region is the country's major source of electricity.

provides the country with its major source of electricity. Its massive concrete wall rises 370 feet (111 meters) high, and is 2,100 feet (636 m) long at its crest. Lake Volta spreads out behind Akosombo Dam; it is the world's largest man-made lake.

From the ledge at the top of the dam wall, you gaze out across the rolling countryside, dotted with small villages and farms. Akosombo is a fitting example of Ghana's will to move into the future and enjoy the benefits of modern technology—but not at the cost of leaving its rich heritage behind.

A young Ga woman, with her child on her back, views the marketplace scene in Accra.

The Road to Recovery

In the last 40 years Ghana has experienced enormous political and economic changes. When it became an independent nation in 1957, all colonial Africa looked to it and its leader, Kwame Nkrumah, as symbols of their own hopes and dreams of independence. A freely elected democratic government, wide-ranging economic development plans, and an energetic leader indicated a bright future for this former colony.

But within nine years the economy was in a shambles and a military dictatorship ruled. Between the 1966 military takeover and the 1992 constitution, Ghana experienced an elected, civilian government only twice, for short periods. Military governments, like that of Jerry Rawlings before he became president, believed that they knew best how to guide the country out of its economic morass.

The long economic decline of the 1960s through the early 1980s had many causes. While a large share of the blame could be placed on government corruption and poor economic management, many of the causes lay outside Ghana. The prices paid in the world markets for cocoa, Ghana's primary export, were so low that the money Ghanaian farmers received for their cocoa sometimes did not cover their costs of growing it.

As a result, farmers suffered and the government was unable to collect taxes and fees for many years. Thus Ghana's health care and education, once the most advanced and far-reaching in Africa south of the Sahara, were reduced to substandard levels by the late 1970s.

In recent years, the economy has been growing again. Cocoa prices have increased, and the government's economic recovery program, which calls for investment in agriculture and better management by the government, has led to a remarkable turnaround for the country's economy. One important result has been the loans from the World Bank and the International Monetary Fund, which have

been put into cocoa production and into developing new industry. In 1992, moreover, Ghana received a new $2.1 billion aid grant from the World Bank.

The most encouraging sign for the country was President Jerry Rawlings's decision, delayed for over a decade, to hold free elections and create a democratic society. Though charismatic and popular, he had lost many supporters who felt that he had failed to keep his key promises to the Ghanaian people. His first term as president was far from tranquil: there were major demonstrations against the government's tax policy in 1995, and more than a thousand people were

These posters urging agricultural development were issued by the Cocoa Planting Board. Cocoa remains the country's main product.

Aluminum ingots are loaded for export at Tema Port.

killed in ethnic fighting in the north in 1993. Yet Rawlings's election to a second term as president seems to indicate that he has regained the nation's trust. As long as the economy can continue to rise and the government's commitment to democracy remains firm, Ghana appears to have a brighter future in store.

A more traditional form of transportation comes to the rescue of a broken-down car near Accra.

‹ G L O S S A R Y ›

Adae   A 40-day period in the Akan calendar. Each year has 9 adaes.

Adinkra   A cotton cloth stamped with symbolic patterns and figures. The adinkra is commonly worn at funerals.

Akpeteshie   A potent alcoholic beverage made from distilled palm wine.

Animism   The worship of spirits that inhabit the earth in various forms.

Cedi   The currency of Ghana. One hundred thirty-six cedis equal U.S. $1.

Coup d'etat   A French phrase, literally "blow against the state," used to describe a takeover of the government and usually effected with sudden violence and armed forces.

Deforestation   Chopping down trees without planting replacements.

Devaluation   The lessening of a currency's value. The Ghanaian government has devalued the cedi in an effort to stabilize the economy.

Fetish   A man-made object believed to be inhabited by a god or spirit. The name comes from the Portuguese word *feticio,* meaning "charm."

Fufu   A popular Ghanaian dish made from yams and plantains.

Golden Stool   The Golden Stool is the symbol of the king's power in many Ghanaian ethnic groups. Asante legend holds that the stool is a gift from heaven.

Harmattan A dry, northeasterly wind that blows across northern Ghana in January and February.

Hausa A trading language spoken by many West Africans.

Kente A traditional Ghanaian cloth made of multicolored threads woven into geometric patterns.

Kontumire A leafy green vegetable similar to spinach.

Mina de Ouro "Gold mine," the name the Portuguese gave to the coastal area of what is now Ghana.

Odwira A week-long festival celebrated by the Akan people at the end of the last adae cycle.

Pirogues Long, narrow, wooden canoes.

Pito An alcoholic beverage brewed from millet.

Polytheism The worship of many gods.

Savanna A grassy plain or flat, open region with few trees.

Scarp A rocky outcropping or steep slope.

Talisman An object worn to attract good luck and to ward off bad luck.

◄INDEX►

PHOTO CREDITS

Edward S. Ayensu: pp. 28, 55, 58 (above), 60–61 (above), 61 (below), 90, 94–95; Jeanie M. Barnett: pp. 16, 40–41, 57, 59 (below), 64 (above); Chicago Mercantile Exchange: p. 52; David Dorsey: pp. 34, 36–37, 48–49, 68; Eliot Elisofon: pp. 62 (above), 63 (below), 64 (below), 77, 78, 87; Porter P. Lowry II: p. 80; Landis Y. McIntire: pp. 2, 13, 14, 18, 20, 23, 26–27, 29, 47, 58 (below), 59 (above, left & right), 60 (below), 62–63 (below), 66, 72, 83, 85, 92, 96, 98; Museum of African Art: pp. 32, 74, 76; New York Public Library: p. 44.

ACKNOWLEDGMENTS

The author and publisher are grateful to these sources for photos and information: Landis Y. McIntire, Janet Milhomme, Beverly Newman, David Williams, Carla Nelson, Godfried Ofori, and Rose Ntim.